For those nights when
it's hard to sleep!

With love
Gill
x

As Night Falls

a bedside
companion

A Lion Book
an imprint of
Lion Hudson plc
Mayfield House, 256 Banbury Road,
Oxford OX2 7DH, England
www.lionhudson.com
ISBN 0 7459 5172 4

First edition 2005
10 9 8 7 6 5 4 3 2 1 0

Acknowledgments
Every effort has been made to trace and contact copyright owners for
material used in this book. We apologize for any inadvertent admissions
or errors, and would ask those concerned to contact us so that full
acknowledgment can be made in the future.

All photographs copyright © Digital Vision, except as noted below.
pp. 14–15, 72–73 copyright © Geoff du Feu.
pp. 26–27, 62–63 copyright © Woodfall Images.
pp. 28–29, 32–33, 34, 37, 56–57, 75, 76–77, 79, 82, 84–85, 86–87, 95,
97, 104, 109, 110–11 copyright © Alamy Ltd.
pp. 45, 58 copyright © Jonathan Roberts.

pp. 16, 25 Scripture quotations taken from the Holy Bible, New Living
Translation, copyright © 1996. Used by permission of Tyndale House
Publishers, Inc., Wheaton, Illinois 60189. All rights reserved.

pp. 33, 34, 43, 53, 62, 73, 83 Scripture quotations taken from the Holy
Bible, New International Version, copyright © 1973, 1978, 1984
International Bible Society. Used by permission of Zondervan and Hodder
& Stoughton Limited. All rights reserved. The 'NIV' and 'New International
Version' trademarks are registered in the United States Patent and
Trademark Office by International Bible Society. Use of either trademark
requires the permission of International Bible Society. UK trademark
number 1448790.

pp. 48–49 Extract taken from 'Immanence' by Evelyn Underhill. Copyright
© 1913 Evelyn Underhill.

p. 67 'Father, you have shown me' by Thomas Merton. Copyright ©
Thomas Merton.

p. 78 'February 2, 1968' from Collected Poems: 1957–1982 by Wendell
Berry. Copyright © 1985 Wendell Berry. Reprinted by permission of North
Point Press, a division of Farrar, Strauss and Giroux, LLC.

p. 86 'My Lord God' taken from Thoughts in Solitude by Thomas Merton.
Copyright © Abbey of Gethsemani.

p. 112 'A Standing Ground' from Collected Poems: 1957–1982 by Wendell
Berry. Copyright © 1985 Wendell Berry. Reprinted by permission of North
Point Press, a division of Farrar, Strauss and Giroux, LLC.

A catalogue record for this book is available
from the British Library

Typeset in 9/12 Americana
Printed and bound in Singapore

As Night Falls

a bedside
companion

Helen Jaeger

A LION BOOK

Contents

For Mum and Dad

Introduction

A few years ago, I visited India and returned very ill. At the time I didn't know that I was going to be ill for over a year, although some deep intuition did tell me that this wasn't a bug that was going to go away in a week or two.

Before my trip, my life had been the usual round of work, family, friends, socializing and church. But my prolonged illness brought me to a new place. Unable to sustain my regular commitments, I watched most of what was inessential fall away.

It wasn't always easy, but truthfully it was an experience of relief and liberation. I was extremely fortunate at the time in that I was receiving excellent care from a medical practice called Interhealth, who at their heart had the principle of holistic care: full health for the whole person – body, mind, spirit and emotions.

Interhealth recognized and trusted to a process of healing that wasn't based simply on drugs and routine. They taught that healing consists of more than bodily health, although it includes this, too. And they gave me the precious gift of unhurried time to get well.

I learned valuable lessons through the time that I was ill. I learned the importance of stillness, patience and grace. I understood how vital following our true vocation in life really is. I grew in trust and relished the pleasure of hiddenness. I was challenged to focus myself, to reach out for what I needed and not to be distracted from my goal of getting well. And the slowness that was a natural consequence of being ill forced me to pay close attention to my immediate environment, where I discovered wonder and the incredible beauty of the seasons, embracing the lesson each season wanted to bring to me. My experience of enforced rest through illness brought about transformation, the lessons of which I continue to practise today, several years after the event. Stillness. True vocation. Focus. Attention. Seasons. Transformation. Grace. Trust. Patience. Hiddenness. These are not idle words or abstract concepts. They are, and can be, lived-in realities, vehicles of the divine in our lives leading us to ever greater life, even when, as faith-bearers, we approach that final life-giver which is death itself. And these are the paths that are described in this book.

There are many ways to use this book, some of which I suggest below. You may like to set aside a deliberate time as you retire to bed, when you can still yourself. Perhaps you will want, each evening, to walk steadily along each of the paths, or maybe you will prefer to skip and jump between them. The important thing is to then walk slowly along your chosen one. Think of your reading and meditation as a gentle evening stroll.

The content of this book is for your benefit, mapping, I hope, paths I and others have travelled and continue to travel. Paths much neglected by current society, but paths of rich fruitfulness and beauty nonetheless. I hope that you enjoy your journey, whichever paths you choose, and that it is a blessing to you.

Suggested ways to use this book

The book is divided into ten paths. Each path has an introductory comment, a Bible passage with ideas for reflection, an imaginative meditation, a prayer, a poem and a range of quotes from, mostly, well-known authors.

Introduction

This is a short section designed to help you begin to think about each particular path. It offers an introduction to the path, with the key features you may like to consider, and is drawn from personal experience.

Meditation

Each Bible passage has been chosen for its relevance to the path in question. Read the passage slowly, allowing any words or thoughts from it to hold your attention. You may like to repeat words or phrases to yourself, allowing them to sink fully into your mind and heart. Do not rush this. Allow the passage to speak to you and your personal situation. You could repeat a phrase or two as you fall asleep.

When you have gleaned all possible nourishment from the Bible passage, you may like to move on to the prompts for reflection attached to it. You could use one or two of these prompts as a way of turning over the passage in your mind and entering into its truths more fully. If particular ideas arrest your attention, make a response to them in whatever way is most suitable for you (for example, a journal or sketch).

Imagine

I suggest that you read through the imaginative meditation first so that you have a good idea of what you are going to be contemplating. When you are ready, close your eyes and use the meditation as a basis for exploring each path more imaginatively and creatively.

Each meditation also has a few questions attached to it. Again, these are designed to help, not hinder, you. You don't have to have an immediate answer to the question, but it may be something that you want to return to in subsequent days, allowing answers and wisdom to come from the deep places within you.

Prayer

Each path has its own short prayer. Speaking another's prayers is effective and restful. If a prayer particularly speaks to you, you may like to copy it out and place it somewhere you can read it easily and spontaneously over a period of time.

Poem

Each path has its own short poem, written from personal experience. Use the poem as the basis of contemplation.

Inspirations

There are quotes included with each path. These quotes
are not random quotes generated by a quote machine!
They have been deliberately chosen for their relevance.
Several of them have found their way out of dog-eared
books onto my walls and notice boards and into my
personal journals over the years. Some quotes have
the ability to sum up what we are thinking and feeling at
any one time. This is the power of words. Allow others'
words to inspire and strengthen you, even as you walk
the paths in this book. The people behind these words
know the reality of the path you are on and are included
in this book deliberately to encourage you. You may like
to place relevant quotes around your home and work
space.

Finally

One last piece of advice: travel slowly and savour what
you find, for it is yours to keep.

Path 1

Stillness

Busy minds

Why is stillness so difficult to achieve? Our bodies can
be at rest, but our minds busy. Or our minds at rest
while our bodies run here and there. We are pulled apart
in many different directions. We feel fragmented, stressed,
pressured, off-balance. And so we try to do more to fix
the problem – which often only makes things worse.

To complicate matters, stillness is not often a virtue
that is praised in our society. On the contrary, we are
actively encouraged to do more and more – by our
families, our religious groups, our employers, the media.
Our culture likes perpetual motion. It likes us to want
much and to do much. But, to our dismay, we find
sooner or later that to have much, to be a consumer,
does not always mean that we will feel fulfilled.
Sometimes our consuming may leave us very empty.
So what is to be done?

Firstly, we must want to let go of our over-activity.
We must desire to be less busy, to have more time, to
appreciate life more richly and more widely. This desire
may grow in us gradually, over time, until we are aware
of a kind of discontent, a restlessness (which is because
we have been without rest). Or it may come to us
suddenly through a crisis, such as an illness or emotional
burnout. We may feel very empty. Recognizing this
emptiness and naming our desire for stillness requires
courage.

And however it comes to us, we may not at first welcome such a desire. We may try to suppress it through further activity or kill it through denying that we have this desire. But to avoid the call to stillness will only complicate and fragment our lives even further. Far better to embrace the call, which, ultimately, is a gift to us and to our world.

It may not be easy, particularly at first. Not to be busy means letting go of the external and internal voices that call, goad, demand and cajole us to perpetual motion. Rarely do we find the one who will say to us, 'It is good to rest.' We are praised for (and judged on) our productivity. Therefore, to find total stillness, total rest, is frequently difficult, sometimes impossible.

We may also need to contend with guilt. If action equals reward, what does non-action equal? What does

our not-doing achieve? When we are judged on fast, quick and visible, the answer is, not much. Over time, the tiny seed of our stillness may well grow into the broad tree that offers shelter. But to begin with, our seed of stillness germinates underground – invisible, unproductive. Is it really worth it?

Yes, of course stillness is worth it. In stillness we find the one who tells us, 'To rest is good.' We find our fragmented minds, emotions and bodies knitting together again. We experience increasing peace and wholeness. We begin to realize, to our great relief and joy, that our identity isn't in all the activity we do, but in our belovedness as sons and daughters of creation. We let go of the false self, who is judged on what we do, and we embrace the real self, who was loved before time began, before we even lifted a finger or sounded a cry.

In stillness, the muddied waters, so long agitated by our permanent activity, finally settle, and we are able to find clarity of mind, heart and intention. And it is from this centred place that we begin to experience a more whole world, because we experience ourselves as more whole.

Meditation

Read

God is our refuge and strength,
always ready to help in times of trouble.
So we will not fear, even if earthquakes come
and the mountains crumble into the sea.
Let the oceans roar and foam.
Let the mountains tremble as the waters surge!

Psalm 46:1–3

Consider

To be really still, most of us need a refuge, as the psalmist describes.

Think about when you have most easily entered into stillness. Can you identify which places, people and practices are your refuges, and where you most easily find stillness? Seek these pools of stillness out at least once a day.

Make regular space for stillness in your life. As you become more deliberate about your intention, so you will notice the benefits of these times of stillness permeating throughout the rest of your life – perhaps in more harmonious relationships or greater creativity.

The psalmist also recognizes that identifying our sources of strength brings confidence and rest.

Think about your sources of strength. What makes you feel strong in a real way (that is, not something which makes you feel fleetingly strong, like an argument with someone)?

Can you name your sources of strength (for example, a hobby, prayer, solitude, friends)?

Celebrate these sources of strength and make time for them in your life. Appreciate and value what gives you strength.

Imagine

Close your eyes. Imagine a stone. Pick it up. Hold it quietly in your hands. Feel it. See it. Weigh it. Turn it over in your

hands. Notice how hard, strong and unbreakable it is. Does it have interesting patterns in it? Take time really to look at and feel the essential quality of the stone you are holding.

What are the rock-like places in you? Perhaps it is your joy or your compassion. Maybe your inner rock, that which is within you that cannot be shaken, is intuition or the ability to know how to help others.

Acknowledge your own inner places of strength and use them for your benefit and the benefit of others.

How can you apply the lesson of stillness to your life right now?

Prayer

O God, you are a refuge and a strength. Help me to find stillness and security in you. You are my rock, stable and unbreakable. Let me rest securely on you, finding peace and wholeness. Amen.

Poem

Still life

When you are still,
The ideas rise,
Whole,
To the surface.

But when you are busy,
The ideas are bro-
Ken, dis-
Persed.

Therefore,
Cultivate stillness.
Shun busyness.

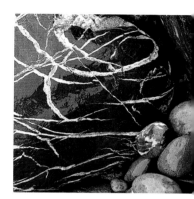

Inspirations

We have to learn to be quiet enough inside ourselves to
listen attentively for that 'light murmuring voice' despite
what is going on outside. That is not too easy to do in an
industrialized western society. There is so much external
noise and bustle going on. There are so many terrible
things happening in the world. Life is lived at such speed.
Changes are always taking place: they happen more
rapidly than they used to in our forebears' time. Noise
from outside penetrates and disturbs us.

Una Kroll

Enlightenment is not an emotion. And it is not a mental
recognition of anything. Perhaps the word that is closest
to it is the realization of stillness, which is when the
mental noise that we call thinking subsides – which is
thinking. There is a gap in the stream of thought, but
there is absolutely no loss of consciousness. In that 'gap'

there is full and intense consciousness, but it has not taken on form. Having access to that formless realm is truly liberating. It frees you from bondage to form and identification with form. It is life in its undifferentiated state prior to its fragmentation into multiplicity. We may call it the Unmanifested, the invisible Source of all things, the Being within all beings. It is a realm of deep stillness and peace, but also of joy and intense aliveness. Whenever you are present, you become 'transparent' to some extent to the light, the pure consciousness that emanates from this Source. You also realize that the light is not separate

from who you are but constitutes your
very essence.

Eckhart Tolle

Contemplation is a country whose centre
is everywhere and whose circumference
is nowhere. You do not find it by travelling
but by standing still.

Thomas Merton

All the troubles of life come upon us
because we refuse to sit quietly for a
while each day in our rooms.

Blaise Pascal

It is folly to pass one's time fretting,
instead of resting quietly in the heart
of Jesus.

St Thérèse of Lisieux

We must cease making our own noise
if we hope to achieve fully the quiet
wisdom of nature and the deep truths
within our hearts. If we continue to
surround ourselves with distracting noise
and push ourselves through constant
movement, we will inevitably keep
craving their opposite. This hunger is
for a silent sanctuary that affords us the
priceless gift of looking at our lives in the relief of stillness,
knowing that simplicity is the real wealth and solitude is good
company. It is as accessible as the next moment, as simple as
being alone.

Richard Mahler

When winds are raging o'er the upper ocean
And billows wild contend with angry roar,
'Tis said, far down beneath the wild commotion,
That peaceful stillness reigneth evermore.

Harriet Beecher Stowe

If only all might be hushed, sense impressions, the soul itself, all imagery, all symbols, all things transient, then we might hear the very voice of the eternal, and if that experience were prolonged, we would indeed enter into the joy of our Lord.

St Augustine of Hippo

I feel that art has something to do with the achievement of stillness in the midst of chaos. A stillness which characterizes prayer, too, and the eye of the storm.

Saul Bellow

Path 2

True vocation

Created for a purpose

To come to rest sometimes feels like entering a season of winter. There are no new plans to form, no new growth to excite us or distant horizons to be conquered. The bareness of nature – plants and trees stripped back to their essential shape and structure – may reflect the bareness we ourselves feel.

Yet this bareness is a tremendous gift. Seeing the shape and structure of a plant or tree is impossible in summer when it is covered in dense foliage. So, too, it is with us. We cannot see our true selves when we are covered with the density of our projects and activities. Without this covering, we are laid bare. But in this laying bare, we gain new insights.

Seeing our essential shape is vital if we are going to choose wisely how to spend our energy. We have limited energy, and to spend it on everything we see around us would mean spending ourselves to the point of exhaustion and beyond.

As we discover our true selves, so, too, we discover our limitations. And limitation, rather than spelling frustration, holds out the gift of liberation. We are liberated from the many false choices we would make if we did not know ourselves so well. Liberated to follow and be all we are, at our very best, able to be.

Wise people have always known this to be true: we are created and designed with purpose and for a purpose. To find this purpose is to find our true vocation. And rest is the friend who can help us to discover and clarify this vocation.

Meditation

Read

After this interview, the wise men went their way.
Once again the star appeared to them, guiding them to
Bethlehem. It went ahead of them and stopped over the
place where the child was. When they saw the star, they
were filled with joy!

Matthew 2:9–10

Consider

Even in darkness, the stars shine. Apparently small
sources of light could lead you on.

In your personal darkness, what stars are beckoning you on?

The wise men journeyed with purpose, following a star
that promised the birth of a new king. Can you name
your purpose – fulfilment, wholeness, healing? What are
you hoping to find at the end of your journey?

Imagine

Close your eyes. Imagine that you are standing in your
kitchen. Look around. Choose an ordinary object such as
a spoon, mug or plate. Pick it up. Think about how it is
shaped and why. In what ways does its function perfectly
match its form?

Can you believe that you have a 'shape' – that you are
designed for a purpose?

Consider your own strengths, likes and abilities. These are part of your 'shape'. Are you expressing them fully? Are there other jobs that you are trying to do for which you are not really designed? Can you let them go and experience the relief of liberation that true humility brings?

How can you apply the lesson of true vocation to your life right now?

Prayer

O God, you created and designed me
    for a purpose.
Help me to discern what that good and noble purpose is. Let everything that is not the essential me fall away. Amen.

Poem

Just the job

Curlew has an unusual beak –
Curved
And unwieldy.

Yet Curlew's beak
Does the job

And makes life
Easy.

Inspirations

Each man has his own vocation; his talent is his call.
There is one direction in which all space is open to him.
Ralph Waldo Emerson

Our business is to love what God would have us do. He
wills our vocation as it is: let us love that, and not trifle
away our time in hankering after other people's vocation.
St François de Sales

For God to explain a trial would be to destroy its purpose,
calling forth simple faith and implicit obedience.
Alfred Edersheim

I don't know what your destiny will be, but one thing I do know: the only ones among you who will be really happy are those who have sought and found how to serve.

Albert Schweitzer

Indeed, man wishes to be happy even when he so lives as to make happiness impossible.

St Augustine of Hippo

Every hardship, every joy, every temptation is a challenge of the spirit; that the human soul may prove itself. The great chain of necessity wherewith we are bound has divine significance; and nothing happens which has not some service in working out the sublime destiny of the human soul.

Elias A. Ford

Plenty of people wish to become devout, but no one wishes to be humble.

François Duc de la Rochefoucauld

There is a medium in all things. There are certain limits beyond, or within, which that which is right cannot exist.

Traditional proverb

If you think you're too small to have an impact, try going to bed with a mosquito in the room.

Anita Roddick

Humility is to make a right estimate of oneself. It is no humility for a man to think less of himself than he ought, though it might rather puzzle him to do that.

Charles Haddon Spurgeon

Humility is the root, mother, nurse, foundation and bond of all virtue.

St John Chrysostom

The secret of life lies in laughter and humility.

G.K. Chesterton

The work of art which I do not make, none other will ever make it.

Simone Weil

Path 3

Focus

Choosing wisely

I once went to watch a falconry display. At the end of the display, members of the audience were invited to hold the hawks and let them fly. I was very excited. I'd always wanted to fly a falcon.

I duly waited in line as small children took their turns before me. Then suddenly I was fitting the falconer's glove over my right hand. The falconer lifted my arm and squeezed a piece of raw meat between my leathered thumb and forefinger. Then he called to the bird, who was sitting on a faraway wall. He called again. And then again.

No swift shadow of a bird flew onto my outstretched arm, as it had for the gleeful children before me. In fact, the bird turned her back on us and instead gazed intently at something beyond the wall. All cajoling, all whistles, all waving of meat scraps: in vain. The bird was not for turning.

While disappointing for me, I admired the falcon's determination. Her focus, her refusal to be distracted from the prey she had undoubtedly spotted on the other side of the wall, was total.

And as I reflected on this incident, it struck me that life needs this level of focus, too. Often we are faced with a myriad of projects and people, all calling, all cajoling, all whistling for our attention. Persuaded by their calls, we can easily lose our focus. Our energy becomes

dissipated, and frustration becomes the companion of our days as we spread ourselves ever more thinly over an ever-widening circle of demands. The solution?

To fix our eyes on a goal and not to be dissuaded from it. To run the race of life steadily, heedless of the calls that would cause us to run here and there, but rarely in the straight line of truth. For focus is the companion of commitment, and commitment is the source of strength which a life of wholeness needs in order truly to flourish.

Meditation

Read

Therefore, since we are surrounded by such a great
cloud of witnesses, let us throw off everything that
hinders and the sin that so easily entangles, and let us
run with perseverance the race marked out for us. Let us
fix our eyes on Jesus, the author and perfecter of our
faith, who for the joy set before him endured the cross,
scorning its shame, and sat down at the right hand of the
throne of God. Consider him who endured such
opposition from sinful men, so that you will not grow
weary and lose heart.

   Hebrews 12:1–3

You were running a good race. Who cut in on you and
kept you from obeying the truth?

Galatians 5:7

Consider

To run a race, you must be as light as possible. What
burdens are you carrying which weigh you down – bad
habits, regrets, grudges? Lay them down and ask God to
help you run your race.

For five minutes simply say the word 'Jesus', or 'peace',
or 'love', in your mind and heart, allowing all other
distracting thoughts to come and go. Use this prayer
whenever you feel pulled apart and need to regain focus.

Does your idea of a race include the idea that God could call you to rest and refreshment?

Who are the 'witnesses' who cheer you on? Identify your sources of encouragement (such as the lives of people you admire) and recall them when you feel you need cheering on.

Imagine

Close your eyes. Imagine that you are a horse at the start of a race. All around you are the crowds: people shouting, cameras flashing. Next to you are other horses: snorting, neighing, shaking their heads. The sights and sounds are overwhelming. Now imagine yourself as the same horse, but with blinkers on. All you can see is the race course set before you. Months of training have accustomed you to your jockey's voice alone. He speaks gently and reassuringly as you attentively listen.

What feelings did each scene give you? What insights did you gain?

How can you apply the lesson of focus to your life right now?

Prayer

O God of my race, help me to run faithfully the path you have set before me. Every day I experience has already been written about in your book of life for me. Help me to know that you are by my side, encouraging me, guiding me and protecting me. Even as I run, may I find rest with you. Amen.

Poem

Inside

I go inside
And inside
Listen.

Too long
I have been
Outside.

This chair,
This rug,
This fire.

From inside
I listen
To the outside.

This chair.
This rug.
This fire.

Close the door
To the outside.

I go in
And inside
Listen.

Inspirations

You must have long-term goals to keep you from being
frustrated by short-term failures.

Charles C. Noble

Our plans miscarry because they have no aim. When a man does not know what harbour he is making for, no wind is the right wind.

Seneca

Perseverance is a great element of success; if you only knock long enough and loud enough at the gate you are sure to wake up somebody.

Henry Wadsworth Longfellow

Many an opportunity is lost because a man is out looking for four-leafed clovers.

Anonymous

A rock pile ceases to be a rock pile the moment a single man contemplates it, bearing within him the image of a cathedral.

Antoine de Saint-Exupéry

Whatever you can do or dream you can, begin it.
Boldness has genius, power and magic in it.
> Johann Wilhelm von Goethe

In the middle of difficulty lies opportunity.
> Albert Einstein

For every mountain there is a miracle.
> Robert H. Schuller

Smooth seas do not make skilful sailors.
> African proverb

Our souls should be directed to God, not merely when we suddenly think of prayer, but even when we are concerned with something else. If we are looking after the poor, if we are busy in some other way or if we are doing any type of good work, we should season our actions with the desire and the remembrance of God.
> St John Chrysostom

Consult not your fears, but your hopes and your dreams. Think not about your frustrations, but about your unfulfilled potential. Concern yourself not with what you tried and failed in, but with what it is still possible for you to do.
> Pope John XXIII

It is my belief that the whole purpose of trying to live a life of prayer is to adore and wait upon God, to listen for that 'light murmuring sound' of God's voice, and to discover what it means for our lives today. God is always faithful, so we are never apart from God: becoming silent and attentive simply helps us to discern what God is doing in us and in the whole of creation.
> Una Kroll

Path 4

Attention

Little things

Slowness, stillness and rest are three great teachers who help us to notice and pay attention to the world around us. Often they quietly and with little fuss open the door to wonder for us.

Paying attention, we see, really see, the uncurling, lime-coloured leaves on a spring tree; we freely inhale the sweet summer scent of an unfamiliar flower in someone else's back garden; we admire the elegant curve of a flock of starlings in flight at dusk.

And we notice something else, too. How those who hurry and rush appear as if in some kind of dream; eyes and minds fixed firmly elsewhere, the beauty of the world, even the urban world, passes them by. They are like passengers on a train travelling through the Alps who refuse to look out of the window. The wonder of the world is lost to them – or rather, they are lost to it. But we who pay attention are not lost. Suddenly a tree in blossom is not merely a tree in blossom. It is hugely and vibrantly alive, the profusion of its blossoms like a silent firework explosion. For a startling moment, we are aware of this creative energy pulsing through everything, including ourselves. To wake up and pay attention like this makes us into mystics, environmentalists, poets and peacemakers.

We are rooted and grounded in wonder and appreciation. In our slowness, we find we are very much alive. We are coming to life, as if waking from a long sleep.

Contemplating the world in this way helps us, as poets have always attested, to contemplate the divine. Furthermore, we discover, to our joy and delight, that the divine is immensely benign. In fact, we discover that the divine is smiling.

Meditation

Read

For this reason I kneel before the Father, from whom his whole family in heaven and on earth derives its name. I pray that out of his glorious riches he may strengthen you with power through his Spirit in your inner being, so that Christ may dwell in your hearts through faith. And I pray that you, being rooted and established in love, may have power, together with all the saints, to grasp how wide and long and high and deep is the love of Christ, and to know this love that surpasses knowledge – that you may be filled to the measure of all the fullness of God.

Ephesians 3:14–19

Consider

Do you consider God to be rich? What difference would it make to you really to grasp this? Could it help you to relax?

Can you offer your inner being to God to be strengthened?

What difference would it make to your life to know that Christ's love for you is wider, longer, higher and deeper than you could ever imagine?

Choose one of the most hurtful experiences of your life, perhaps something you find very difficult to get over. Remembering that Christ's love for you is far greater than you could ever begin to imagine, can you ask to see this experience from his perspective?

Imagine

Close your eyes. Imagine yourself as a plant in a pot. You feel constrained, restless, weary. You are pot-bound. Now imagine tender hands removing the pot from around you. You are placed in moist, warm soil. Your roots can relax and stretch out. There is room to grow, light, food, water and all the nutrients you need to be healthy. The hands that removed you from the pot will continue to look after you.

How did you feel as you were removed from your pot to the ground – scared, nervous, excited? How did you feel knowing that you were going to be looked after?

How can you apply the lesson of attention to your life?

Prayer

O gardener God, you take delight in all your creation, including me. Please plant and establish me in the rich soil of your love so that, lacking nothing, I may grow and flourish, rooted always in you. Amen.

Poem

Fresh as a daisy

Before enlightenment
The heart
Is a black bud
Tightly
Closed.

When enlightenment comes,
The heart
Flings off its black petals,
Becomes
A daisy.

We are surrounded
By a hundred million wonders.

Inspirations

Wonder is the basis of worship.
Thomas Carlyle

Stuff your eyes with wonder... live as if you'd drop dead
in ten seconds. See the world. It's more fantastic than any
dream made or paid for in factories.
Ray Bradbury

God moves in a mysterious way,
His wonders to perform;
He plants his footsteps in the sea,
And rides upon the storm.
William Cowper

The world will never starve for want of wonders, but for want of wonder.
> G.K. Chesterton

He who can no longer pause to wonder and stand rapt in awe is as good as dead; his eyes are closed.
> Albert Einstein

Life can be seen through your eyes, but it is not fully appreciated until it is seen through your heart.
> Mary Xavier

Rest strengthens the body, the mind too is thus supported; but unremitting toil destroys both.
> Ovid

Live your life each day as you would climb a mountain. An occasional glance toward the summit keeps the goal in mind, but many beautiful scenes are to be observed from each new vantage point. Climb slowly, steadily, enjoying each passing moment; and the view from the summit will serve as a fitting climax for the journey.
> Harold V. Melchert

Be aware of wonder. Live a balanced life – learn some and think some and draw and paint and sing and dance and play and work every day some.
> Robert Fulghum

The real voyage of discovery consists not in seeking new landscapes, but in having new eyes.
> Marcel Proust

I come in the little things,
Saith the Lord:
Not borne on morning wings
Of majesty, but I have set my feet
Amidst the delicate and bladed wheat
That springs triumphant in the furrowed sod.
There do I dwell, in weakness and in power;
Not broken or divided, saith our God!
In your strait garden plot I come to flower:
About your porch my vine
Meek, fruitful, doth entwine;
Waits, at the threshold, Love's appointed hour.

I come in the little things,
Saith the Lord:
Yea! on the glancing wings
Of eager birds, the softly pattering feet
Of furred and gentle beasts, I come to meet
Your hard and wayward heart. In brown bright eyes
That peep from out the brake, I stand confessed.
On every nest
Where feathery Patience is content to brood
And leaves her pleasure for the high emprize
Of motherhood –
There doth my godhead rest.

I come in the little things,
Saith the Lord:
My starry wings
I do forsake,
Love's highway of humility to take:
Meekly I fit my stature to your need.
In beggar's part
About your gates I shall not cease to plead –
As man, to speak with man –
Till by such art
I shall achieve my immemorial plan,
Pass the low lintel of the human heart.
Evelyn Underhill

Earth's crammed with heaven,
And every common bush afire with God;
But only he who sees takes off his shoes –
The rest sit round it and pluck blackberries.
Elizabeth Barrett Browning

Path 5

Seasons

Rhythm of life

Many of us live without seasonal awareness, particularly in the glass and concrete canyons of the city. Here, our lives are geared towards constant productivity. We have lost our struggle to maintain a sense of right rhythm in our lives, and believe we are the sole instigators, captains and sustainers of our destinies. Rather than enlarging us, this diminishes us. But if we immerse ourselves in the seasons, we learn a different and valuable lesson.

Winter comes to us with her dark nights and crystal stars (even in the urban orange). The earth rests from its activity. All appears dead. So winter brings us to the thresholds of rest and faith. We navigate by stars, as wise people have done in the past, to discover new life and new miracles. We dream, with our eyes wide open and tightly shut. We welcome light in darkness and appreciate more fully the enlightenments we have received. We sleep, in faith that spring always follows winter, life always follows death. And we trust that our rest is an important part of the cycle of life, looking both backwards and forwards to the busy seasons of autumn and spring.

Spring arrives. The new growth around us, fragile but resolute, mirrors our own burgeoning projects and ideas, which have hibernated safely in us over the winter season. We seed the activities that we hope will come to fruition in coming months. And we welcome the beautiful, tender blossoms that speak of a harvest to come.

Then summer is with us, with her long days of light. In its fullness, everything rests again. Trees and flowers are in their full glory. We celebrate our relationships and the gifts of our physical bodies as we play outside.

Autumn comes, bearing in her arms the fruits we diligently planted several months previously in spring. We enjoy and give thanks for the fruit of our work and lives, preserving some of it perhaps for the future winter months, when we will be at rest again.

And so it is. The cycle of life turns and invites us to be carried on it – we who have chosen to travel in faith and gratitude.

Meditation

Read

The moon marks off the seasons,
and the sun knows when to go down.
You bring darkness, it becomes night,
and all the beasts of the forest prowl.
The lions roar for their prey
and seek their food from God.
The sun rises, and they steal away;
they return and lie down in their dens.
Then man goes out to his work,
to his labour until evening.
How many are your works, O Lord!
In wisdom you made them all;
the earth is full of your creatures.

Psalm 104:19–24

Consider

Can you see the design behind the way the
seasons work?

What special gifts do you find in each season,
or would you like to find in each season?

Can you see any seasons in your own life? What
name would you give to the season you are
going through at the moment?

Imagine

Close your eyes. Choose a room in your house which you use frequently. How could you bring an awareness of the seasons into it? What could you see in that room that might tell you about the season? What colours would there be... what decorations... what objects... what pictures... what smells?

Here are some ideas to help you:

> Bring natural objects from outdoors into your home: pebbles from a beach holiday; a pumpkin in autumn; bare twigs from winter trees; spring blossom in a vase.

> Create a picture or wall hanging, drawing on the colours and shapes of the seasons (for example, black and white for winter, or pastels for spring).

> Choose poetry, writing or Bible readings that speak of a particular season. Pin them up where you can read them every day.

> Grow something from seed.

Try to imagine the room fully finished. Now imagine what you would do to make it look that way. If you wish, you could make some notes or sketches. It doesn't have to be a grand plan – just something simple, but meaningful.

How can you apply the lesson of the seasons to your life right now?

Prayer

O creative God, you turn the earth and you created the seasons. Everything you do is wonderful and wise. Help me to live in the rhythms of the seasons you have placed in my life: to find the treasures of each time you have marked out for me. Thank you that you are a God of beauty and order. Please grant me your wisdom, that I may know how to live well. Amen.

Poem

Harvest moon

From behind a rock,
You rose.

Huge, orange
In a Prussian blue sky.

Awesome sister
Who turns the tides,

I say to you:
We share a mystery.

Like you,
I am harvesting
At night,
In darkness.

Like you,
I am harvesting,

Before autumn equinox
Tilts the world to winter.

Inspirations

In a way winter is the real spring, the time when the inner
things happen, the resurge of nature.
Edna O'Brien

Therefore all seasons shall be sweet to thee,
Whether the summer clothe the general earth
With greenness, or the redbreast sit and sing
Betwixt the tufts of snow on the bare branch
Of mossy apple tree, while the nigh thatch
Smokes in the sun-thaw; whether the eave-drops fall

Heard only in the trances of the blast,
Or if the secret ministry of frost
Shall hang them up in silent icicles,
Quietly shining to the quiet moon.
Samuel Taylor Coleridge

We grow great by dreams. All big men are dreamers. They see
things in the soft haze of a spring day or in the red fire of a long
winter's evening. Some of us let these dreams die, but others
nourish and protect them; nurse them through bad days till they
bring them to the sunshine and light which comes always to
those who hope that their dreams will come true.
Woodrow Wilson

Given, not lent,
And not withdrawn, once sent,
This infant of mankind, this One,
Is still the little welcome Son.
New every year,
Newborn and newly dear,
He comes with tidings and a song,
The ages long, the ages long;
Even as the cold
Keen winter grows not old,
As childhood is so fresh, foreseen,
And spring in the familiar green.
Sudden as sweet
Come the expected feet.
All joy is young, and new all art,
And he, too, whom we have by heart.

Alice Meynell

I trust in nature for the stable laws
Of beauty and utility. Spring shall plant
And autumn garner to the end of time.
I trust in God – the right shall be the right
And other than the wrong, while he endures.
I trust in my own soul, that can perceive
The outward and the inward – nature's good
And God's.
Robert Browning

A child kicks his legs rhythmically through excess, not absence, of life. Because children have abounding vitality, because they are in spirit fierce and free, therefore they want things repeated and unchanged. They always say, 'do it again'; and the grown-up person does it again until he is nearly dead. For grown-up people are not strong enough to exult in monotony. But perhaps God is strong enough to exult in monotony. It is possible that God says every morning 'do it again' to the sun; and every evening 'do it again' to the moon. It may not be automatic necessity that makes all daisies alike; it may be that God makes every daisy separately, but has never got tired of making them. It may be that He has the eternal appetite of infancy; for we have sinned and grown old, and our Father is younger than we. The repetition in Nature may not be a mere recurrence; it may be a theatrical encore.
G.K. Chesterton

Rest is not idleness, and to lie sometimes on the grass under trees on a summer's day, listening to the murmur of the water, or watching the clouds float across the sky, is by no means a waste of time.
Sir John Lubbock

Every season hath its pleasure;
Spring may boast her flowery prime,
Yet the vineyard's ruby treasuries
Brighten autumn's sob'rer time.
Thomas Moore

To us also, through every star, through every
blade of grass, is not God made visible if we will
open our minds and our eyes.

Thomas Carlyle

In the midst of winter, I found there was, within
me, an invincible summer.

Albert Camus

Spring unlocks the flowers to paint the laughing
soil.

Bishop Reginald Huber

The bee from her industry in the Summer eats
honey all winter long.

Belgian proverb

Winter is an etching, spring a watercolour,
summer an oil painting and autumn a mosaic
of them all.

Stanley Horowitz

Path 6

Transformation

Becoming

To contemplate transformation is to enter holy and unpredictable ground. This desire, like none other, speaks to the radical in us, because transformation requires nothing less than total commitment and total surrender. Only commitment and surrender can carry us through the potential upheavals of transformation. This is wild country, often arduous, rarely gentle.

So what brings us to this radical and risky place? For some, it's a growing dissatisfaction with how their life is lived. For others, it's a realization that there is more, deeper, more widely to be savoured. And for yet others, a sense of ennui or boredom drives them to the frontier land between what was and what can be.

And so it is that we fling our arms wide open to the universe and say: do with me as you will. Or often the universe flings open its arms and says to us: come on a journey with me to unfamiliar land.

And so it is that we give ourselves over, as Alcoholics Anonymous puts it, to a 'higher power'. We surrender. We submit. To ask for transformation is rarely greedy, often humble, especially if we put our hand firmly into the hand of the divine – and keep it there.

And what happens when we do? I'd like to say that your world won't be shaken, but I can't promise it. We learn new ideas – about ourselves, our world, God. We grow as people, with God's help, in love and charity and hope. Old certainties may lose their light, but always with our moral compass we gain new heights. We may cry and groan as the old world passes away, but we move into new life. In a sense, we do truly move from glory to glory, even if the transition is not always smooth, but frequently painful.

True transformation isn't about a change of clothes, car or hairstyle. It isn't about a new relationship or a new job. It's about the heart. And the fruits of true transformation? Greater wholeness, greater serenity, greater purpose. We slough off the dead skin of our old, bad habits and live as new and newly-becoming people, beacons of light for a creation that cries out for the very transformation it sees us experiencing.

The circumstances of our lives may change. Then again, they may not. But we are forever changed and, with God's grace and our continued surrender, forever better.

Meditation

Read

Now the Lord is the Spirit, and where the Spirit of the Lord is, there is freedom. And we, who with unveiled faces all reflect the Lord's glory, are being transformed into his likeness with ever-increasing glory, which comes from the Lord, who is the Spirit.

2 Corinthians 3:17–18

Consider

When and where have you felt most free, most alive and most whole?

What looks like freedom may not end up being freedom at all. How can you be wise in choosing the paths of freedom?

It has been said that the Holy Spirit is like the sun. He shines on everyone, but not everyone receives his warmth and power. How can you open yourself more to the Spirit of the Lord?

Are there any areas in your life that feel cold and damp? Maybe you can let the Spirit shine on them and warm them.

Imagine

Close your eyes. Imagine that your face has been turned away from the sun, in shadow. Now turn to the sun. Let yourself rest and relax in its rays. See how your body and mind both relax. Watch as your skin takes on a healthy glow. The sun is God's light shining on you, transforming you. Allow yourself to be rested, changed and warmed. The only effort you need make is to be still. Sometimes the best prayer is simply to bask in God's love.

What feelings did you have as you lay still in God's love: completely open, completely still? How could you incorporate this practice into your life? Would you like to?

How can you apply the lesson of transformation to your life right now?

Prayer

O bright, shining God, I turn from all my darkness and come into your gentle light. I lie down before you, completely open. Shine on me and change me, as I rest in your love. Let me become radiant and healthy as your Spirit brings me true freedom. Amen.

Poem

Storm warning

Today,
A storm-day,
I walk
The water-fashioned rocks.

I, too,
Have been cut
And shaped
By waves.

Inspirations

It is easy to want things from the Lord and yet not want the Lord himself, as though the gift could ever be preferable to the giver.

St Augustine of Hippo

One day an angel visited the farmyard and told the animals that the baby Jesus had been born in Bethlehem. All the animals were very excited by the news, and talked about the different things that they could give the baby. The horse said, 'I can give him my strong back to ride on'; the dog said, 'I can guard him with my barking'; the sheep said, 'I can keep him warm with my fleece'; the only one who couldn't think of anything to give was the worm.

It felt very sad as it wriggled its way to Bethlehem. The other animals told Jesus of their gifts and he blessed them. Then the worm came along last of all and said, 'I am very sorry. I have no gift. All I can give you is myself as I am.'

'But that is the greatest gift of all,' said Jesus, and he touched the worm, and it began to glow with light.

Anonymous

Jesus, your love is the dearest
of all that is most sweet.
You take hold of our minds
with your love;
you possess us so clearly
because you make us despise
all transitory things,
and yearn marvellously
for what you desire.
You came to me,
and every corner of my heart
has been filled with the lovely sound
of your joy.

Richard Rolle

Batter my heart, three-personed God; for you
As yet but knock, breathe, shine, and seek to mend;
That I may rise, and stand, o'erthrow me, and bend
Your force, to break, blow, burn and make me new.
I, like an usurped town, to another due,
Labour to admit you, but O, to no end.
Reason, your viceroy in me, me should defend,
But is captived, and proves weak or untrue,
Yet dearly I love you, and would be loved fain,
But am betrothed unto your enemy,
Divorce me, untie, or break that knot again,
Take me to you, imprison me, for I
Except you enthrall me, never shall be free,
Nor ever chaste, except you ravish me.
John Donne

Hope has two beautiful daughters, Anger and Courage.
Anger at the way things are and Courage to see that they
do not remain the way they are.
St Augustine of Hippo

Father, you have shown me how to walk in your
footsteps. You are daily transforming me. My heart is filled
with joy as you renew and refresh me. You now call me
your beloved just as you called Jesus your beloved Son.
You have shown me that I am worthy to be called
one of your children. Your love for me surpasses my
comprehension. Now you are calling me to come closer
to you. You are challenging me to a new level of growth.
Give me the desire in my heart to rise up and meet this
challenge. This I pray in the name of our Lord Jesus.
Amen.
Thomas Merton

Father, I abandon myself into your hands; do with me
what you will. Whatever you may do, I thank you. I am
ready for all, I accept all. Let only your will be done in
me and in all your creation – I wish no more than this, O
Lord. Into your hands I commend my soul. I offer it to
you with all the love of my heart, for I love you, Lord, and
so need to give myself, to surrender myself into your
hands, without reserve, and with boundless confidence,
for you are my Father.

Charles de Foucauld

When our lives are focused on God, awe and wonder
lead us to worship God, filling our inner being with a
fullness we would never have thought possible. Awe
prepares the way in us for the power of God to transform
us, and this transformation of our inner attitudes can
only take place when awe leads us in turn to wonder,
admiration, reverence, surrender and obedience toward
God.

James Houston

The last and highest result of prayer is not the securing
of this or that gift, the avoiding of this or that danger. The
last and highest result of prayer is the knowledge of God –
the knowledge which is eternal life – and by that
knowledge, the transformation of human character, and of
the world.

George John Blewett

To do for yourself the best that you have it in you to do –
to grit your teeth and clench your fists in order to survive
the world at its harshest and worst – is by that very act to
be unable to let something be done for you and in you
that is more wonderful still. The trouble with steeling
yourself against the harshness of reality is that the same
steel that secures your life against being destroyed
secures your life also against being opened up and
transformed by the holy power that life itself comes from.
You can even prevail on your own. But you cannot
become human on your own.

Frederick Buechner

Path 7

Grace

All is well

We like to believe that we are the sole controllers of our lives. The huge variety of choice surrounding us, both in our relationships and our material possessions, leads us to believe that it is up to us, and us alone, what happens in our lifetimes.

Seduced by this idea, we find ourselves in an ever-increasing myriad of choices. Nothing is settled, everything is in flux. Even our feelings are not accurate barometers of our destinies, changing as they do from moment to moment, from mood to mood.

The choices that were meant to liberate us now enslave us. Our days are filled with endless talk of fundamental change – houses, jobs, relationships – and how we can begin to bring this change about.

Blinded in this way by the piles of choices stacked high before us, we fail to discern a deeper reality at work. We forget – and forget to appreciate – the ways our lives have been carried, shaped and supported by others than ourselves. In our self-sufficiency, we forget, and may begin to refuse, grace.

But grace is the great unconditional lover who supports and sustains us. Often it is only in great crisis or difficulty that we call out to this hidden support; only when confronted by our weakness and neediness that we realize that we need more – more than our simple self

can provide. Yet even as we are calling, we are answered. We find, to our astonishment and humbling, that grace has been there all along – helping us, providing for us and waiting to be involved in our lives.

Our lives, if we let grace in, can have a beautiful shape and pattern not woven merely by our own skill. Grace finds for us what we truly, deeply need. No, perhaps not the new relationship, the new job, the new house. But more precious things.

Grace can grant us, if we need it, wisdom, insight, freedom and belonging. Grace roots us in this life in great love and showers us with acceptance. Grace allows us, we who like to think that we control the whole universe, the ability to be like little children, the ability not to know, the ability, in short, to rest – but resting always in the arms of omniscient love.

Meditation

Read

The eternal God is your refuge,
and underneath are the
everlasting arms.
He will drive out your enemy
before you,
saying, 'Destroy him!'
So Israel will live in safety alone;
Jacob's spring is secure
in a land of grain and new wine,
where the heavens drop dew.

> Deuteronomy 33:27–28

I will lie down and sleep in peace,
for you alone, O Lord,
make me dwell in safety.

> Psalm 4:8

Consider

What are your current refuges? Are they good
refuges – strong, protective, storm-proof? Or
poor refuges – weak, leaky, draughty?

What would it mean to make God your
refuge? Can you trust that God is good?

What difference would it make to you to
know that God wants you to live in safety?
How could this help you to relax?

Repeat Psalm 4:8 to yourself as you go to
sleep.

Imagine

Close your eyes. Imagine yourself falling, falling, falling. As you fall, all your desires, wants and dreams spin past you. Suddenly you are caught in strong arms. You are held securely. You can catch your breath and, if you like, bury your face in the chest of the one who has saved you. You allow yourself to be held and loved.

What did it feel like to stop? To be held and to be loved? This is what God wants to do for you. Bring this to mind every time you start to feel out of control, panicked or worried.

How can you apply the lesson of grace to your life right now?

Prayer

O God of the strong arms, sometimes I want to be held by you and sometimes I don't. I don't always understand my conflicting feelings about this, but help me to trust you more and more. Help me to understand that your every thought and desire towards me is for my welfare. Amen.

Poem

Whispers of strength

The eagle thought
It was very strong.

But the wind beneath
Its wings whispered,

'I am stronger.'

Inspirations

I am lying down tonight as
    beseems
in the fellowship of Christ,
Son of the Virgin of ringlets,
in the fellowship of the gracious
    Father of glory,
in the fellowship of the Spirit of
    powerful aid.
I am lying down tonight with God,
and God tonight will lie down with
    me.
I am lying down tonight with the
    Holy Spirit,
and the Holy Spirit this night will lie
    down with me.
I will lie down this night with the
    Three of my love,
and the Three of my love will lie
    down with me.

    Gaelic prayer

O Lord, Almighty God, open wide
my heart and teach it by the grace
of your Holy Spirit to ask for what
is pleasing to you. Direct my
thoughts and senses so to think
and to act that by a worthy
manner of life I may deserve to
obtain the eternal joys of the
heavenly kingdom. Direct my
actions according to your
commands so that, ever striving to
keep them in my life, I may receive
for my deeds the eternal reward.
Amen.

    Saint Bede the Venerable

There is no single definition of holiness; there are dozens, hundreds. But there is one I am particularly fond of; being holy means getting up immediately every time you fall, with humility and joy. It doesn't mean never falling into sin. It means being able to say, 'Yes, Lord, I have fallen a thousand times. But thanks to you I have got up again a thousand and one times.' That's all. I like thinking about that.

Dom Helder Camara

God says to every one of us what Paul says to his disciples, 'I do not want what is yours, but you.'

Raniero Cantelamessa

The soul of one who loves God always swims in joy, always keeps holiday and is always in the mind for singing.

St John of the Cross

In the dark of the moon, in flying snow, in the dead of winter, war spreading, families dying, the world in danger, I walk the rocky hillside, sowing clover.

Wendell Berry

Sweet Jesu,
your body is like a meadow
full of scented flowers and health-giving herbs;
in just this way your body is full of wounds,
sweetly aromatic for a devout soul
and as health-giving as herbs for each sinful person.
Now, sweet Jesus, I implore you,
allow me the sweet aroma of mercy
and the health-giving medicinal prescription
of grace.

Richard Rolle

I sought my soul
But my soul I could not see.
I sought my God
But my God eluded me.
I sought my brother
And I found all three.

Anonymous

Reflect on your present blessings, of which every man
has many; not on your past misfortunes, of which all men
have some.

Charles Dickens

Life is at its noblest and its best when our effort
cooperates with God's grace to produce the necessary
loveliness.

William Barclay

He that hath the grace of God hath wealth enough.

William Shakespeare

God obviously has no need of the products of your busy
activity, since he could give himself everything without
you. The only thing that concerns him, the only thing he
desires intensely, is your faithful use of your freedom.

Teilhard de Chardin

Of all the thoughts of God that are
Borne inward into souls afar,
Along the psalmist's music deep,
Now tell me if that any is
For gift or grace surpassing this –
'He giveth his beloved sleep'?

Elizabeth Barrett Browning

Path 8

Trust

Being community

We find it hard, if we are honest, to trust fully. We have all, in various ways, experienced betrayal and being let down. Even the best of our relationships falter and need to be mended by forbearance and forgiveness – although perhaps, ultimately, this is what makes them the best.

Trust is not always easy to achieve. We grow accustomed, are trained even, to expect disappointment and failure. We expect to be gossiped about. We learn that no one, truly, is the steadfast friend we long for and need.

Or do we? Can we not, at some point in our lives, choose to move from this narrow and pessimistic view of the human condition to one that is warmer, more generous? Can we not remember the countless times others have helped us, nurtured us, strengthened us? Can we not deliberately call to mind the kindness of strangers and the seemingly random acts of thoughtfulness and care we all experience every day?

Yet still we don't want to trust fully like this, because trust, in some way, implies dependence. And we like to believe that we are independent and in control. We give up such ideas with difficulty. Yet such narrowness of vision leads only to isolation.

Dependence does not diminish us; rather, it increases both us and the one depended on. We connect. We interrelate. We do not say to another, 'You are responsible for me,' but we do say, 'You matter to me.'

As we do this, we find to our joy that true community, respecting and nurturing individuality while recognizing our need for each other, is born and grows.

In true community we discover more of ourselves, much more than if we had stayed in our self-sufficient, fearful isolation. Yes, in trust we may fall, but we are caught. We allow ourselves to be caught, to be supported. And this gives joy to the hearts of both the faller and the catcher, the receiver and the giver.

Trust opens our hearts to others. Yes, we must choose carefully whom we trust. But not trusting, we risk staying small, closed and unfulfilled.

Meditation

Read

Do not be anxious about anything, but in everything, by prayer and petition, with thanksgiving, present your requests to God. And the peace of God, which transcends all understanding, will guard your hearts and your minds in Christ Jesus.

Finally, brothers, whatever is true, whatever is noble, whatever is right, whatever is pure, whatever is lovely, whatever is admirable
– if anything is excellent or praiseworthy –
think about such things. Whatever you have learned or received or heard from me, or seen in me
– put it into practice.
And the God of peace will be with you.

Philippians 4:8–9

Consider

We are all surrounded by care and nurture throughout
our lives. Take time at the end of your day to stop and
deliberately think about the positive things that are
happening, regardless of whatever generally difficult or
good situation you are passing through.

What causes you unpeace and distress? Do you dwell
unhealthily on these things?

Consider how your nightly routine may make it
difficult for you to relax or rest. How can you set your
mind on true, noble, right, pure, lovely, admirable things
more often?

Cultivate a positive attitude of prayer and thanksgiving.

Imagine

Close your eyes. Slowly remember each and every time someone has supported you or cared for you. Maybe it was the phone call, the card, the prayer or the flowers. Perhaps it was the babysitting, the money or the meal. Imagine each act filling your heart with thankfulness. Now see the hand that has poured this goodness into your life. That hand is God's.

How can you apply the lesson of trust to your life right now?

Prayer

O God of abundance, you love to give, generously and graciously. You delight to give to me. Help me to trust you, to freely depend on you. You have everything I need in the palm of your hand. You are the most faithful friend and lover of my soul that I will ever find. I give up my narrow, self-sufficient ways and joyfully accept your help. Amen.

Poem

Light bearer

The sun
Is bright
On her face,
Cleansing her mind.

She closes
Her eyes
And makes
For the tide line,

Guided
By light.

Inspirations

I do not seek to understand that I may believe,
but I believe in order to understand.

St Anselm of Canterbury

Lord Jesus, it is the greatest possible joy that you
are highest and mightiest, noblest and most
honourable, lowest and humblest, most familiar
and courteous. And truly you will show us all this
marvellous joy when we shall see you. And you
want us to believe this and trust, rejoice and
delight, strengthen and console ourselves, as
we can, with your grace and help, until the
time that we see it in reality. For the greatest
abundance of joy which we shall have is this
wonderful courtesy and familiarity of our Father,
who is our creator, in you, our Lord Jesus Christ,
our brother and our saviour.

Julian of Norwich

My Lord God, I have no idea where I am going. I
do not see the road ahead of me. I cannot know
for certain where it will end. Nor do I really know
myself, and the fact that I think that I am following
your will does not mean that I am actually doing
so. But I believe that the desire to please you
does in fact please you. And I hope I have that
desire in all that I am doing. I hope that I will
never do anything apart from that desire. And I
know that as I do this you will lead me by the
right road, though I may know nothing about it.
Therefore will I trust you always, though I may
seem to be lost and in the shadow of death. I will
not fear, for you are ever with me, and you will
never leave me to face my perils alone.

Thomas Merton

God provides for him that trusteth.
George Herbert

Faith is a higher faculty than reason.
Philip James Bailey

Faith is putting all your eggs in God's basket, then
counting your blessings before they hatch.
Ramona C. Carroll

Order your soul; reduce your wants; live in charity;
associate in Christian community; obey the laws;
trust in providence.
St Augustine of Hippo

The love I bear Christ is but a faint and feeble spark, but it is an emanation from himself: he kindled it and he keeps it alive; and because it is his work, I trust many waters shall not quench it.

John Newton

If we are walking in joy, we are trusting God.

Anonymous

Live by what you trust, not by what you fear.

Anonymous

I know God won't give me anything I can't handle; I just wish he didn't trust me so much.

Mother Teresa of Calcutta

Trials are medicines which our gracious and wise
physician prescribes because we need them; and
he proportions the frequency and weight of them to
what the case requires. Let us trust his skill and thank
him for his prescription.
    Isaac Newton

Path 9

Patience

The power of waiting

Hurry. Rush. Scramble. Achieve. Now. Must.

We live in an impatient culture. We are both impatient with ourselves and impatient with others. We demand and expect everything now. Yet again, impatience jolts us out of sync with the rhythms of the world.

Further, impatience burdens us. It is a heavy load always to be demanding so much of ourselves and of others. But we carry the load, because we've come to value impatience over patience. We curse the parcel for arriving late, the meeting for being postponed, the flight for being delayed. And others curse us for our apparent poor planning, for our disorganization, for our tardiness. We live in a cycle of impatience, both generating it and receiving it.

Such impatience is not gentle, kind or loving. Such a state of stimulation, prolonged as it often is, is hardly good for us. The constant inner turmoil, clenched fists and weakened health do us no favours. So why do we value impatience so highly?

Impatience gets results. Or so we've been led to believe. Impatience achieves. Impatience makes us feel good, strong, in control, powerful. The shout of impatience, surely, is the most powerful of all.

Or is it? Does impatience really achieve so much? Faced ourselves with an impatient person, do we feel like helping them – or hindering them? More likely, if we're honest, it's the latter.

And so we discover, even belatedly, that patience is what we need. Patience opens the way for us to be creative, not harassed. Patience allows us space to be and to breathe. Patience gently gives us the chance to think, to come up with genuine solutions that are not forced or haphazard.

Patience is the soil in which the seeds of our best dreams, left undisturbed, grow and become visible. It is the water that softens the hardest rock. So patience, far from being powerless, is immensely productive.

To hurry and rush erodes our sense of self and well-being. To be patient connects us to the greater rhythms of life, to forces more benign and more powerful than we can imagine, to solutions more creative, to healing more profound. Patience achieves all this – and barely raises a whisper.

Meditation

Read

But the fruit of the Spirit is love, joy, peace, patience, kindness, goodness, faithfulness, gentleness and self-control.

Galatians 5:22–23

Through patience a ruler can be persuaded, and a gentle tongue can break a bone.

Proverbs 25:15

The end of a matter is better than its beginning, and patience is better than pride. Do not be quickly provoked in your spirit, for anger resides in the lap of fools.

Ecclesiastes 7:8–9

Consider

If your life were a fruit bowl, which spiritual fruits would it be most full of? Which least full of? Can you ask God to help you display all the fruits of the Spirit?

When have you seen patience prevail in a situation where anger has not succeeded?

Are there problems in your life that you want to solve quickly? How does that make you feel – tense, frustrated? Can you allow yourself to be patient?

Imagine

Close your eyes. Imagine a beautiful fruit tree. It is autumn. Its branches are heavy with luscious, ripe fruit. A person is hurrying past the tree. They are muttering, frowning, wringing their hands. Suddenly they stop. They look up at the tree and pluck a juicy fruit from its branches. They take a mouthful. It is the most succulent, juiciest, sweetest fruit that they have ever tasted. Amazement spreads across their face. Feelings of delight, joy and peace fill their body. They take another bite, and then another. They sink to the ground beneath the tree's branches and continue to eat the fruit, now more slowly, savouring every mouthful.

Which did you identify with more: the tree, or the impatient person?

If you identified with the tree, are you willing to let any and everyone who needs to eat the fruit of your spiritual life? Enjoy God's pleasure in you as a fruitful person.

If you identified with the impatient person, can you imagine God as the fruitful tree? Can you come and take what is freely offered – perhaps the gift of patience?

How can you apply the lesson of patience to your life right now?

Prayer

O gracious God, you are the most patient person of all. With patience and wisdom you made the universe. With patience and wisdom you planned redemption. With patience and wisdom you designed me and planned my life, so that no suffering was wasted and no joy lost. Let me enter into the rhythms of your patience, trusting that ultimately you make all things well. May patience bring peace to my life and joy to my heart. Amen.

Poem

Breathe

Patience
Has lengthened
My days.

Waiting
Has given me
Air
To breathe.

I fling my arms
Wide
And touch

Nothing.

I fill my lungs
And the sky
Is not emptied.

Inspirations

The tree of life my soul hath seen,
Laden with fruit, and always green;
The trees of nature fruitless be
Compared to Christ the apple tree.

For happiness I long have sought,
And pleasure dearly I have bought;
I missed of all, but now I see
'Tis found in Christ the apple tree.

I'm weary with my former toil,
Here I will sit and rest awhile;
Under the shadow I will be
Of Jesus Christ the apple tree.

This fruit doth make my soul to thrive,
It keeps my dying faith alive;
Which makes my soul in haste to be
With Jesus Christ the apple tree.

Traditional Shaker hymn

We resign into your hands our sleeping bodies, our cold hearths and open doors. Give us to awaken with smiles, give us to labour smiling. As the sun returns in the east, so let our patience be renewed with the dawn; as the sun lightens the world, so let our loving kindness make bright this house of our habitation.

    Robert Louis Stevenson

Lord, teach me the art of patience while I am well, and enable me to use it when I am sick. In that day either lighten my burden or strengthen my back. Make me, who so often in my health have discovered my weakness in presuming on my own strength, to be strong in my sickness when I solely rely on your assistance.

    Thomas Fuller

Good Jesus, strength of the weary, rest of the restless, by the weariness and unrest of your sacred cross, come to me who am weary, that I may rest in you.

    E.B. Pusey

How poor are they that have not patience! What wound did ever heal but by degrees?

    William Shakespeare

Have courage for the great sorrows in life and patience for the small ones. And when you have laboriously accomplished your daily task, go to sleep in peace. God is awake.

> Victor Hugo

> Let nothing disturb you,
> nothing afright you.
> All passes away.
> God only shall stay.
> Patience wins all.
> Who has God lacks nothing.
>
> St Teresa of Avila

The world is a looking-glass and gives back to every man the reflection of his own face. Frown at it and it will in turn look sourly upon you; laugh at it and with it, and it is a jolly kind companion.

> William Makepeace Thackeray

O God, make us children of quietness and heirs of peace.

> St Clement of Alexandria

The work will wait while you show your child a rainbow, but the rainbow won't wait while you do the work.

> Patricia Clifford

Dear Lord and Father of mankind,
Forgive our foolish ways;
Reclothe us in our rightful mind,
In purer lives thy service find,
In deeper reverence praise.

In simple trust like theirs who heard,
Beside the Syrian sea,
The gracious calling of the Lord,
Let us, like them, without a word,
Rise up and follow thee.

O sabbath rest by Galilee,
O calm of hills above,
Where Jesus knelt to share with thee
The silence of eternity,
Interpreted by love!

With that deep hush subduing all
Our words and works that drown
The tender whisper of thy call,
As noiseless let thy blessing fall
As fell thy manna down.

Drop thy still dews of quietness
Till all our strivings cease,
Take from our souls the strain and stress,
And let our ordered lives confess
The beauty of thy peace.

Breathe through the heats of our desire
Thy coolness and thy balm;
Let sense be dumb, let flesh retire;
Speak through the earthquake, wind and fire,
O still small voice of calm.

John Greenleaf Whittier

Path 10

Hiddenness

Beneath the surface

We live in a culture that lauds and applauds celebrity.
To be in the public gaze is seen as the highest
achievement, the best virtue. No matter for what –
exposure is everything.

And of course, in a culture with this value, to
be obscure is death. Witness the countless celebrities
who try to resurrect their careers – their exposure – by
whatever means possible. Obscurity, hiddenness, is
anathema. Recognition comes only from others, even
if they are a million strangers reading a newspaper.

So what happens when we are taken away from
the public world, perhaps voluntarily, as Thoreau and
countless hermits have done, or involuntarily through
illness? Our lives, by choice or necessity, become more
hidden. We are thrown on our own resources. We are
forced to go inside and contemplate what we find there.

Such a journey is a fearful prospect. Yes, it may well
turn out to be an epic journey, where the hero, ourselves,
must face alone the inner monsters and attempt to defeat
them. No wonder we try to avoid such a journey.

But avoidance is no real solution. Our fears, our
inner monsters, persist. Our lives remain fragmented,
fearful, unwhole. There is – and always has been – only
one solution: to go through.

We must face and conquer those monsters, those
fears, perhaps, of aloneness or unworthiness. We must

muster our courage and decide, resolve, to face what keeps us from a life that is hidden. And we find, in that very decision, that the battle is half won.

But what is it about hiddenness that is worth the struggle, worth the fight? Hiddenness is not about losing our worth; it's about finding it and discovering that it is held in a far safer hand than the fickle fingers of fame.

Hiddenness is about discovering wealth, like unmined seams of precious gems, running through our very depths. We discover treasure, vast swathes of it, in ourselves, placed there millennia ago by a benign hand. Instead of ugliness, we discover beauty. Instead of mourning, we discover our capacity for laughter, celebration and gratitude. Yes, hiddenness is worth the journey. Our jewels are of inestimable worth and forever ours. And it is hiddenness alone that reveals these treasures and yields them up to us.

Meditation

Read

How great is your goodness,
which you have stored up for those who fear you,
which you bestow in the sight of men
on those who take refuge in you.
In the shelter of your presence you hide them
from the intrigues of men;
in your dwelling you keep them safe
from accusing tongues.
Psalm 31:19–20

The kingdom of heaven is like treasure hidden in a field.
When a man found it, he hid it again, and then in his joy
went and sold all he had and bought that field.

> Matthew 13:44

I will give you the treasures of darkness,
riches stored in secret places,
so that you may know that I am the Lord,
the God of Israel, who summons you by name.

> Isaiah 45:3

Consider

What treasures have you already found in unexpected
places or situations?

Think about a time or place that seemed most unpromising.
Can you identify anything positive that came from that
time or place?

Darkness can seem like a hostile place, but the psalmist
recognizes that God hides those he loves in his presence.
If you feel that you are in darkness at the moment, can
you re-envision it as a welcome place, a place of safety
for you?

Imagine

Close your eyes. Imagine that you are mining for precious jewels by hand. You dig through hard earth. It's unrewarding, back-breaking work. Sweat pours down your face. Now imagine that your spade hits something crunchy. It bring up jewels mixed with mud. You dig further: there's more. You wash the jewels in water and enjoy the glint of their beautiful colours in the sunshine. All your hard work has been rewarded.

What insights did you gain as you imagined this scene?

Can you see yourself as the earth and the jewels as your inner treasures: peace, joy, laughter, compassion, kindness, celebration, wisdom, insight – whatever those unique riches are in you.

Can you enjoy the rewards of your hard work?

How can you apply the lesson of hiddenness to your life right now?

Prayer

O God of treasure, you have hidden rich and beautiful things in me. Please bring them to light, so that I and my world may enjoy them. Sometimes the spiritual life seems like back-breaking work – hard and unrewarding. But then you surprise me with treasure. Help me to take time to stop and appreciate the beautiful gifts you have given me. Amen.

Poem

Heron

Lying
In the tall grass
Flattened,

I spotted you.

Blue grey
In foliage.

The Saturday crowds
Were intent, bent
Over two terrapins
On a log
In the pond.

Heron,
I will not disclose
Your presence

If you
Will not disclose mine.

Inspirations

The deeds God loves most are those he alone has
witnessed.

Rafaella Mary

The work an unknown good man has done is like a vein
of water flowing hidden underground, secretly making the
ground green.

Thomas Carlyle

Happiness lies in our own back yard, but it's probably well hidden by crabgrass.

Anonymous

The aspects of things that are most important to us are hidden because of their simplicity and familiarity.

Ludwig Wittgenstein

To be satisfied with a little is the greatest wisdom; and he that increaseth his riches increaseth his cares; but a contented mind is a hidden treasure, and trouble findeth it not.

Akhenaton

Everything in nature contains all the powers of nature. Everything is made of hidden stuff.

Ralph Waldo Emerson

Men talk of 'finding God', but no wonder it is difficult; he is hidden in that darkest hiding place, your heart. You yourself are a part of him.

Christopher Morley

Guard well within yourself that treasure, kindness. Know how to give without hesitation, how to lose without regret, how to acquire without meanness.

George Sand

You will tell me that I am always saying the same thing: it is true, for this is the best and easiest method I know; and as I use no other, I advise all the world to it. We must know before we can love. In order to know God, we must often think of him; and when we come to love him, we shall then also think of him often, for our heart will be with our treasure.

Brother Lawrence

An inner reality is equally important to an outer reality.

Gloria Steinem

If we go down into ourselves, we find that we possess exactly what we desire.

Simone Weil

Everything is gestation and then bringing forth.

Rainer Maria Rilke

Feeling is deep and still; and the word that floats
    on the surface
Is as the tossing buoy, that betrays where the anchor
    is hidden.

Henry Wadsworth Longfellow

However just and anxious I have been,
I will stop and step back
from the crowd of those who may agree
with what I say, and be apart.
There is no earthly promise of life or peace
but where the roots branch and weave
their patient, silent passages in the dark;
uprooted, I have been furious without an aim.
I am not bound for any public place,
but for ground of my own
where I have planted vines and orchard trees,
and in the heat of day climbed up
into the healing shadow of the woods.
Better than any argument is to rise at dawn
and pick dew-wet red berries in a cup.

Wendell Berry